ROBERT BADEN-POWELL

by Julia Courtney

For a free color catalog describing Gareth Stevens' list of high-quality children's books, call 1-800-341-3569 (USA) or 1-800-461-9120 (Canada).

Exley Publications would like to thank the Scout Association of Great Britain, the World Association of Girl Guides and Girl Scouts, and Wing Commander John King for their invaluable help in preparing this book.

Picture Credits

Wing Commander John King, *Baden-Powell, A Family Album* by Heather Baden-Powell — 42, 43; Boy Scouts Association of South Africa — 31, 51; Boy Scouts of America — 59 (both); Daily Mirror — 36; Mary Evans — 24; Nick Birch, Exley Publications Picture Library — 4 (upper), 15, 18-19, 22, 26, 32 (both), 34 (both), 39 (both), 47 (four at right); Fine Art Picture Library — 8 (lower), 27; Girl Guides Association of Great Britain — 40, 45, 49; © Karalee Helminak, 1990 — 67; National Army Museum — 12, 16; National Film Archive — 13; Pictorial Nostalgia — 41; Popperfoto — 17, 20, 52, 53; Retrograph Archive Collection — 14; The Scout Association of Great Britain — 4 (lower), 10, 21, 28, 29, 30, 33, 37, 54 (lower), 54-55 (large), 55 (lower), 57 (both); Brian Souter — 6, 8 (upper), 9 (reproduced by kind permission of the Headmaster, Charterhouse); World Association of Girl Guides and Girl Scouts (WAGGGS) — 55 (upper); World Scout Bureau — 46-47 (large), 58.

North American edition first published in 1990 by
Gareth Stevens Children's Books
RiverCenter Building, Suite 201
1555 North RiverCenter Drive
Milwaukee, Wisconsin 53212, USA

First published in the United Kingdom in 1990 with an original text © 1990 by Exley Publications Ltd. Additional end matter © 1990 by Gareth Stevens, Inc.

Library of Congress Cataloging-in-Publication Data

Courtney, Julia.
  Robert Baden-Powell / by Julia Courtney.
    p. cm. — (People who have helped the world)
    Summary: Examines the lifetime achievements of the man who founded the Boy Scout movement in Great Britain and saw it expand all over the world.
  ISBN 0-8368-0214-4
    1. Baden-Powell of Gilwell, Robert Stephenson Smyth Baden-Powell, Baron, 1857-1941—Juvenile literature. 2. Boy Scouts—Great Britain—Biography—Juvenile literature. [1. Baden-Powell of Gilwell, Robert Stephenson Smyth Baden-Powell, Baron, 1857-1941. 2. Boy Scouts—Great Britain.] I. Title. II. Series.
  HS3268.2.B33C68   1990   90-30229
  369.43'092—dc20   [B]   [92]

Series conceived and edited by Helen Exley
Picture research: Diana Briscoe
Editors: Samantha Armstrong and Margaret Montgomery
Series editor, U.S: Rhoda Irene Sherwood
Research editors, U.S.: Scott Enk and John D. Rateliff

Printed in Hungary

1 2 3 4 5 6 7 8 9 96 95 94 93 92 91 90

ROBERT BADEN-POWELL

The man who created the international Scouting movement that gives young people opportunities to excel

by Julia Courtney

Gareth Stevens Children's Books
MILWAUKEE

*Above: The Copse, or
small wood, in which
Robert Baden-Powell
played as a boy.
Already a talented artist,
he painted this picture as
a pupil at Charterhouse,
whose buildings can be
seen in the background.
Robert revelled in the
chance to explore the
woods and fields.*

The watcher in the wood

Crouched under a thick tangle of briars lay a red-haired boy of thirteen. He was watching a rabbit in a nearby clearing, its ears ready to detect any unusual sound in the wood. Suddenly the rabbit sat upright, looked around, and disappeared between the trees.

What had it heard? Must be hostile Indians! Surely they had not spotted the fire he had made; he had been careful to make very little smoke. Almost silently the boy came out of his hiding place and stealthily climbed the smooth trunk of a beech tree, concealing himself among the leaves. He would be safe now — it was amazing how rarely anyone thought of searching above eye level. The cracking of twigs which had alerted the rabbit came nearer; enemies were definitely approaching and the fugitive held his breath.

"I could swear one of those young rascals came in here," whispered one "enemy warrior" to the other. "If I catch him he'll be in trouble for [going out of] bounds."

"Well, there's nothing to be seen now," his colleague replied. "Let's get back or we'll be late for afternoon lessons."

The "hostile Indians" were really two masters from Charterhouse, a British boys' boarding school whose playing fields bordered a secluded wood known locally as the Copse. As they made their way back across the fields, Robert Stephenson Smyth Baden-Powell slid down from his tree and prepared to follow them. Perhaps he, the intrepid Indian scout, could creep along under the cover of the hedgerows so silently that those dangerous enemies would not detect him.

The year was 1870. Queen Victoria was on the throne of Great Britain and thirteen-year-old Robert Baden-Powell (known to his friends as B-P) was

Opposite, below: B-P's love of nature inspired him to make outdoor discoveries and adventures the basis of early Scouting. This love has been passed through every generation of Boy Scouts, Girl Scouts, and Girl Guides. This modern photograph captures the same feeling of inspiration.

5

Wearing distinctive caps and straw hats, Charterhouse students of 1872 pose for a group photograph outside their newly erected school buildings. Robert Baden-Powell, on the far right, was deeply attached to his school. Nicknamed "Guts," he was happy during his years there; as an adult he often came back to visit, and kept in touch with school friends throughout his life.

being educated at Charterhouse, in the county of Surrey, in southeastern England. Formal lessons were the part of school life that interested B-P least.

His mother would be horrified when she received notes from the headmaster. He would write such remarks as "Seems to take very little interest in his work," "Pays not the slightest attention," and "Has to all intents given up the study of mathematics."

"Your son's ability is greater than would appear by the results," the headmaster would explain when she inquired about B-P's progress.

What B-P learned

B-P's real education was taking place in that wooded thicket where he stalked animals, watched birds, and acted out stories of action and adventure.

"It was here," he wrote later, "that I imagined myself a backwoodsman, a trapper, and an Indian scout. I used to creep about warily looking for a sign and getting close-up observations of rabbits,

squirrels, rats and birds. . . . What I picked up in the Copse was both a preparation and a pursuit.

"The Copse lore . . . went beyond the development of health of body and mind — it helped me as a youngster to find my soul. It was an elemental way, but that solitary creeping and 'freezing' in observation of the birds and beasts and the butterflies made one a comrade instead of an interloper in the family of nature, it brought some realization of the wonders that surround us, and it revealed too, through open eyes, the beauties of the woods and sunsets."

B-P lived at a time when men, particularly upper-class Englishmen, were not expected to talk much about their innermost beliefs. During his life, B-P rarely got closer than this to expressing his feelings about the oneness of humankind and the natural world. It was his belief in such oneness that enabled him to dedicate his life to young people less fortunate than himself. He realized that sharing his belief in this oneness could be done through the fun of outdoor games and make-believe.

A determined mother

B-P's father, Professor Baden Powell, was a clergyman and an eminent scientist, a colleague of the most famous biologists, physicists, and botanists of the day. He was more than twenty years older than his second wife and, at the time of their marriage, was already a widower with four children.

Families were large in Victorian days. By the time the professor died in 1860, there were seven more children: Warington, then aged thirteen; George, twelve; Augustus, eleven; Francis, nine; Robert (B-P), three; Agnes, the only girl, eighteen months; and Baden, three weeks. Sadly, three more children had died as babies, and Augustus died when only thirteen.

Although far better off than many Victorians, the Powells* were far from rich and when B-P's mother, Henrietta, was widowed, she knew she would have a struggle to educate her brood.

*After September 21, 1869, the Powells became the Baden-Powells.

"A young man who was thrilled by thoughts of adventure had little time for his studies. [B-P's] reports at Charterhouse were outstandingly poor but, since it was 'bad form' to work hard, would have been rated out-standingly good by the boys."
Tim Jeal, in his biography, Baden-Powell

Above: The grounds and buildings of Charterhouse.

Right: As this picture suggests, nineteenth-century children wore stiff clothes and had formal manners. Like the family pictured here, the Baden-Powells moved in social circles where achievement and success mattered. Left with a large, fatherless brood, Henrietta Baden-Powell became concerned about preparing her sons for their future careers.

8

But Henrietta Powell was a born fighter. She was also quite a gifted artist, as her husband had been. She taught all of her children the virtues of hard work and perseverance, along with the basics of reading and writing. They also learned to share. The children never had pocket money or a personal allowance; instead there was a communal cash box from which each family member withdrew money as needed, with a note explaining how much had been taken.

A gifted child

Young B-P, growing up in the middle of this large, lively family, idolized his elder brother Warington, who was training to go to sea in the Merchant Service. In turn, Agnes and little Baden looked up to B-P as their big brother who could construct toys from unlikely odds and ends and make kites to fly in the park near their London home.

B-P was happy to play with the younger children, but he also liked to be alone to read. He could also pick out tunes on any musical instrument he could lay his hands on, and he especially enjoyed painting and drawing. But rather than praise her son's versatility, Henrietta was worried when she noticed him using a pencil and brush equally well in either hand — or even in both hands at once!

At this time Robert's other great talents began to emerge. He clearly had tremendous potential as an actor, singer, and comedian. He began writing his own comedy sketches and learned all the hit songs of the day.

Needless to say, Henrietta Baden-Powell did not envisage the precarious and, at that time, rather disreputable career of an actor, or even an artist, for one of her sons. She hoped that Charterhouse, the prestigious school to which B-P won a scholarship in 1870, would train him to be a Victorian gentleman.

But B-P lived mainly for school plays, soccer games, and his adventures in the Copse. As he grew older he shared outdoor vacations with his older brothers, Warington, George, and Frank. They hiked, they canoed, and they sailed in a yacht designed by Warington. On board this craft, B-P, as the youngest, was made cabin boy, cook, and dishwasher. His

"Throughout his life [B-P] would work with tireless energy at whatever project or objective he had in hand. At school his ambition had been to be admired and popular. Yet to be popular, one had to appear not to be trying too hard."

Tim Jeal, in his biography, Baden-Powell

The Charterhouse shooting team of 1874 with B-P, age sixteen, third from the left. He was an active member of this team for three years. While in the army he qualified as a shooting instructor and, later, actively encouraged schools to include shooting in their sporting timetable.

Robert Baden-Powell, leaving school. A parent who wanted to send his son to Charterhouse once asked the headmaster, "I want you, Sir, to assure me that the boys who come to your school are the sons of gentlemen." "Well, they always leave gentlemen," answered the headmaster proudly.

cooking was disastrous but improved after Warington insisted on his consuming his burnt pea soup: "Frank," he warned, "will sit by and see that you eat the whole of that muck yourself!"

Choosing a career

Of course, B-P was expected to follow family tradition and go to Oxford University. But to his mother's indignation, he was turned down.

Nineteen years old and rather uncertain about what to do next, B-P noticed a newspaper announcing an examination for entrance into the army. Successful candidates would become officers in either the infantry or cavalry and would serve in India. Growing interested, B-P read on: "mathematics, English,

French, geography, free-hand drawing." He would try his luck. For twelve hot July days, B-P battled with a variety of tricky examination questions.

When the results were published, he was amazed to find that he had come in fifth out of 718 candidates. His mother was jubilant. What a mistake those Oxford dons had made about her clever son!

For the first few years as a cavalry officer, B-P would not earn much, but the family worked together to provide Sub-Lieutenant R. S. S. Baden-Powell with the many things he would need in his new life. On October 30, 1876, they gathered to wave good-bye as he set sail for India.

"By appearing to be more brilliant and capable than everyone around him, [B-P] managed to convey an impression of supreme self-confidence."

Tim Jeal, in his biography, Baden-Powell

Lieutenant Baden-Powell

So Baden-Powell's army career began. He would be a soldier for over thirty years, and during this period he would develop many of the ideas that later surfaced in the Scouting movement.*

With the exception of two years spent in England on sick leave, B-P spent his first eight years in the army as a junior officer in India. At this time no actual fighting was occurring, so the chief enemies of the garrison were disease and boredom.

B-P excelled at the sports enjoyed by the young officers, especially polo. He saved his money until he was able to buy a pony named Hercules. Despite being bony and ugly, Hercules soon learned to be an excellent polo pony, and B-P went on to fund sporting expenses by training and selling other ponies.

Besides sports, amateur theatricals were a passion with the soldiers stationed in remote parts of India. Baden-Powell was in great demand. After all, he could sing, act, tell jokes, and paint scenery — with both hands at once!

Baden-Powell was also progressing with his training as an officer. In June 1878, at age twenty-one, he was awarded a "first class" in his final exams and was promoted to the rank of lieutenant.

*Some nations, including Canada, use the term *Scouts* for the boys' organization and *Girl Guides* for the girls'. In the United States, the groups are referred to as *Boy Scouts* and *Girl Scouts*.

But shortly afterward, he became chronically ill, and exactly two years after arriving in India, B-P returned to England and spent 1878-80 on sick leave.

Afghanistan

On October 5, 1880, Lieutenant Baden-Powell, now twenty-three years old and back to full health, sailed from England to rejoin his regiment. It had been sent to Afghanistan, to the northwest of India, where the British had become involved in a civil war over who was to rule. Here his new commanding officer was Colonel Baker Russell. Baden-Powell described him as "a character, and no mistake! . . . He was the sort of man you would think twice about trifling with, and you would be right."

Colonel Russell had an unorthodox approach to soldiering: "He was in no way guided by the drill book and knew little and cared less for the prescribed words of command." Baden-Powell had always felt instinctively that drill and parades did no one any good, and now he had a colonel who agreed with him.

On patrol

Colonel Russell brought out the initiative and self-reliance of his men. He decided that B-P should join a small team responsible for examining the wild terrain over which a recent battle had been fought. B-P would scout ahead to learn as much as possible that might be of military use. To do this, he would need keen eyes and the ability to make quick, accurate sketches in the open air. His mapmaking skills would be used to the fullest.

When he returned from this exciting three-day expedition, further reconnaissance work came his way. He spent many nights on mounted sentry duty. B-P had graduated from the make-believe of the Copse to the deadly earnestness of army life.

Already, a few of B-P's drawings and articles had appeared in newspapers and magazines; now he resolved to accomplish something more impressive. *Reconnaissance and Scouting*, his first book, appeared in 1884. It discussed exploring and mapping hostile country, and included accounts of expeditions to examine enemy movements and strongholds.

British troops patrolling dangerous frontier territory needed to remain ever watchful and alert. Stationed in Africa and India, Baden-Powell devised special training for recruits serving in war-torn areas. This training later formed the basis of Scout activities.

Baden-Powell had arrived in India as an eager but inexperienced teenager. In 1884, at age twenty-seven, he sailed away from Bombay a tough, seasoned army captain. He spent the next thirteen years with the British army in various parts of Europe and Africa and published several books.

In this time, he became a self-controlled and often a silent man. His strength lay in his ability to include his men in all important decisions and to earn their respect and fondness.

In love with Africa

It was Africa that made the greatest impression on Baden-Powell. He loved the continent and admired its people. Right from the start of his army career, he had studied the local languages wherever he went. In this way he got to know people of the various African nations. He respected these people both as allies and as opponents.

Perhaps the greatest African warrior people were the Zulus, and Baden-Powell never forgot his first impression of a Zulu *impi*, or army, on the march. He recalled, "I heard a sound in the distance which at first

Zulu warriors on the march — an impressive spectacle that Baden-Powell never forgot: "The time-keeping and rhythm of these warriors in their singing was marvellous," he wrote in 1888, "accompanied as it was with the stamping of the feet and booming and rattling at given periods: a glorious sound." Years later the discipline and physical prowess of the Zulus were a major inspiration for the campfire choruses and rituals of the Scouting movement.

In this picture, present-day Zulus are reconstructing Zulu warfare as B-P would have seen it.

I thought was an organ playing in church and I thought for a moment we must be approaching a mission station over the brow of the hill.

"But when we topped the rise we saw moving up towards us from the valley below three long lines of men marching in single file and singing a wonderful anthem as they marched. Every now and then one man would sing a few notes of a solo which were then responded to by an immense roar of sound from the whole impi, of deep bass voices and higher tones singing in harmony."

Quickly B-P wrote down the tune and, as far as he could understand them, the words: "Eengonyama! Gonyama! Invooboo! Ya-boh! Ya-boh! Invooboo!" Years later he would teach those words to a group of boys seated around a campfire in the very different setting of the English countryside.

"The wolf that never sleeps"

Baden-Powell's Zulu friends were greatly impressed by his courage and alertness. He was proud of the

The popular image of B-P as an intrepid soldier, already sporting the characteristic broad-brimmed hat and short mustache. This portrait appeared on the front cover of a lively piano piece written to commemorate his exploits in South Africa.

special names they gave him, all of which summed up significant aspects of his personality:

• *M'hlalapanzi*, "the man who lies down to shoot," with the further meaning of "the man who lays his plans carefully before shooting them into practice";

• *Kantankye*, meaning "he of the big hat." Like many people with red hair, B-P tended to get sunburned, so he always wore the broad-brimmed hat he had used during his first tour of duty in South Africa, in 1884-85. This hat became his trademark, and was to be part of the early Scout uniform;

• *Impeesa*, the name he was most proud of, which means "the wolf that never sleeps." Baden-Powell regarded this name as the greatest compliment that he had ever received.

In 1897, Baden-Powell returned to India. By now forty years old and a full colonel, he served for two years as commander of the Fifth Dragoon Guards stationed on India's troubled northwest frontier.

As regimental commander, Baden-Powell was fully responsible for the training of his men and was eager to put some of his ideas into practice. So he decided to work out a plan for training the new recruits. They had arrived from Britain with a good basic education but, in B-P's words, "without individuality or strength of character, utterly without resourcefulness, initiative or the guts for adventure."

Moreover, Baden-Powell was convinced that strict, formal military training did nothing to develop these qualities, so he drew on his own past experiences to evolve a more flexible method.

The fleur-de-lis, originally an emblem used by the kings of France but later used as a badge for B-P's trained army scouts. The famous fleur-de-lis logo later became a timeless symbol linking Colonel Baden-Powell's original educational ideas with the worldwide Scouting movement of today.

A new type of training

Perhaps the most revolutionary aspect of Colonel Baden-Powell's training was his determination that his men should *enjoy* it. He divided the recruits into small groups. Then he delivered entertaining lectures to them, full of jokes and stories about his experiences in scouting and reconnaissance. Then the men had to put theory into practice by going out alone or in pairs on observation exercises.

Those who passed all the tests earned the title of "Scout" and were given a special arm badge, the fleur-de-lis ("flower of the lily"), or north point. It is

In the dust and heat of India, Colonel Baden-Powell saw that British troops regularly endured the relentless drilling of army discipline. He did not agree that parade-ground smartness and slavish obedience to orders were all-important, and courted official disapproval by reducing petty rules and rigid ceremonial.

based on the design used to indicate north on a map or compass and also represents the shape of the iris. A few years later, the Scouting organization was to make it one of the world's best-known symbols.

Baden-Powell recorded many of these ideas on training and outdoor activities in another book, *Aids to Scouting*. This soon became his most successful publication, but B-P was too preoccupied to take much notice of its unexpected popularity.

In May 1899, after two years in India, B-P returned home on leave. He planned to return to his regiment in India before the end of the year. But after only two weeks, he was ordered back to South Africa, where Britain's empire was being threatened by the Dutch settlers, the Boers. War seemed inevitable.

At the beginning of July, Colonel Baden-Powell sailed for South Africa and the testing experience that was to make him a national hero.

Mafeking

Arriving in South Africa, Baden-Powell was given the strategically placed town of Mafeking as his base. This normally quiet town was on the front line between the rival forces — the British army and the tough, independent Boers. It also served as the main supply depot for the local British troops.

Standing on the Molopo River in Cape Colony, Mafeking was without defenses of any kind. As it became apparent that war could not be prevented and that there would be a siege of the town, Colonel Baden-Powell set about fortifying it. He had great respect for his resourceful Boer opponents.

Without delay, he organized the building of an underground shelter for protection from enemy shelling. Willing hands dug trenches. Carts and wagons were sacrificed to barricade the roads.

A guarded train took many of Mafeking's women and children to safety in the southern town of Kimberley. Baden-Powell sat in his headquarters above a lawyer's office and reviewed the situation. He knew that danger threatened the remaining nine thousand people of Mafeking — and the poorly equipped British garrison of 1,250 men was no match for the Boers.

Tough, self-reliant Boer farmers learned to ride and shoot at an early age, and they knew every inch of the harsh terrain covered by their wagons. They were more than a match for less experienced British soldiers. Colonel Baden-Powell never underestimated these formidable opponents. He realized that his troops might do better behind the defenses of Mafeking than to risk trying to defend themselves in the open country that the Boers knew so well.

Siege

Preparations were barely completed by October 11, 1899, when war was declared. On October 13, a force of nine thousand Boers surrounded the town. The siege of Mafeking had begun.

Three days later, a rain of shells struck the town. For four hours, explosions ripped up the roads and littered the market square with shrapnel.

But when the townsfolk inspected the damage, little harm had been done. B-P scribbled a wry message to British headquarters — "All well. Four hours' bombardment. One dog killed." He handed it to a local man with instructions to make sure the Boers "accidentally" saw it on the way.

In the following days he continued bluffing the Boers, managing to convince them that the defending force was far better equipped than it really was. During the night, to prevent night attacks, two men

An original historic photograph of Mafeking; there were only black-and-white photographs at that time, so this one has been hand-tinted. It shows the five-inch (13-cm) howitzer gun, nicknamed "The Wolf." It was made in the town's own railroad workshops during the siege and possessed a greater range than any other gun in the town. The Wolf was in action against the Boers throughout March 1900, but finally burst while the men were attempting to shoot a record distance.

would run across the town flashing the gas company's single homemade searchlight, giving the Boers the impression that Mafeking was surrounded by a chain of searchlights.

A little light relief

For the first few weeks of the siege, Baden-Powell knew little about what was going on outside Mafeking. Any reports he did receive were unreliable, based on hearsay. Realizing it could be some time, possibly months, before help arrived, he took over the running of essential services and introduced food rationing.

By now the South African summer was beginning, and to supplement the strict rationing that he had imposed, Baden-Powell urged the local people to grow their own fruit and vegetables. They also kept

the trenches in good repair and patched up the red clay buildings damaged by constant enemy gunfire.

B-P, always full of energy, knew that both soldiers and civilians needed some light relief from the tension of the siege. Hostilities ceased on Sundays, so each Sunday, after a church service, everyone enjoyed "sports, baby shows, concerts, theatricals, and fooleries of every kind" dreamed up by the commanding officer himself.

While he presented a lighthearted exterior, Colonel Baden-Powell took his responsibilities seriously. The men had confidence in his strength and determination. At night he lived up to his African name, Impeesa, the Wolf that Never Sleeps. Under cover of darkness he would creep out of the town to inspect the enemy lines and find out what the Boers were doing.

Colonel Baden-Powell stands on the far left of a group which includes both army officers and civilian engineers.

Inside the besieged town, meanwhile, the young boys were becoming a menace. Exuberant and high-spirited, they got in everybody's way as the adults tried to cope with the grim realities of the siege.

Even worse, the boys courted danger, going into the bomb shelters only at the last possible moment and often popping out again before the "all clear" signal sounded. The fear of being blown up was forgotten in the race to collect fragments of exploded shells for souvenirs.

Colonel Baden-Powell could see that the boys had to become a help rather than a hindrance. With all the men busy with war work, many vital jobs around the town were left undone. One of B-P's officers, Major Lord Edward Cecil, was told to organize a new cadet force for boys over the age of nine.

The Mafeking Cadet Corps

He started with a group of eighteen boys, made up of one sergeant major, one sergeant, two corporals, and fourteen privates. They were highly pleased when khaki uniforms were scrounged from the military stores. Major Cecil taught them discipline and drill

Opposite: Pictured here is a woman we know only as Mrs. Davies, one of the women who remained in Mafeking to help defend the town. An expert shot, she was able to take a turn at the barricades, while other women braved enemy gunfire to tend casualties suffering the horrible effects of shelling.

Below: The Mafeking Cadet Corps contributed directly to the formation of the Scouting movement by proving to Baden-Powell that, given proper training, boys could show courage in a tough situation. Here the corps, which undertook postal deliveries and other vital jobs, lines up proudly outside a war-damaged building.

21

B.G.LENNON&C°

Photographed during the Mafeking siege, Lennon's Chemist Shop (pharmacy) shows extensive damage from enemy shells. Few of Mafeking's buildings escaped unscathed, but thanks to the flimsy mud construction of many houses, shells were able to pass straight through the walls without detonating until they hit the ground some distance away. Also, since only one building in town had more than one storey, people were unlikely to be trapped in falling rubble.

and, using games and contests, prepared them for the jobs they were to do.

Baden-Powell was impressed by the cadets' thoroughness and courage. They were soon ready to take over responsibility for carrying messages, delivering mail, and taking turns at the lookout posts.

In time, the Mafeking Cadet Corps was officially recognized as part of Mafeking's defenses. Perhaps the cadets' proudest moment came when the town ran out of stamps, and together the local photographer and the printer of the *Mafeking Mail* produced some sets for temporary use. On the stamps was a picture of the cadets' sergeant major, on his bike, smartly preparing to deliver the letters.

Years later, Baden-Powell remembered them. The cadets had shown him that young boys could stay cool and efficient in a dangerous situation and that they could handle responsibility. The Mafeking Cadet

Corps was, in fact, a vital link in a chain of events that would eventually lead to the founding of the worldwide Scouting movement.

Anxious days

Although morale remained high, largely because of B-P's outward calm and confidence, time was running out for the citizens and the garrison of Mafeking. Christmas 1899 came and went. As the new century opened, thousands of British soldiers arrived in South Africa. Hopes of help soon reaching Mafeking rose. But they were dashed when, in February, Colonel Baden-Powell heard that it would be May before troops would arrive.

Supplies of food, money, and ammunition were now running low. As usual, B-P was full of ideas. He organized the printing of Mafeking's own bank notes and set up four large soup kitchens. These dispensed stew made to the following recipe: "Half a horse, 250 pounds; mealie meal, 15 pounds; oat husks, 47 pounds. This makes 132 gallons of soup the consistency of porridge." Sowens, a kind of oat porridge, became the staple diet but was so tasteless that everyone welcomed an unexpected swarm of locusts. Eaten fried, these were said to have "all the aroma and subtlety of chewed string," but B-P managed to find a small supply of curry powder which slightly improved the taste.

After six months, exhausted messengers began to reach Mafeking with news of the war, with long-delayed mail from families and friends, with a message to Baden-Powell from Queen Victoria herself. "I continue watching with confidence and admiration the patient and resolute defence which is so gallantly maintained under your ever resourceful command," she wrote. But still no help arrived.

It was the end of April. The siege had lasted for almost two hundred days. Food supplies would be exhausted within the next four weeks, and sickness was spreading among soldiers and townspeople alike. Baden-Powell summoned his staff and told them that the rations must be further reduced. He was determined that the British wouldn't give in.

But how much longer could Mafeking hold out?

"Not a day has passed since the siege began but they have not thrown shrapnel and common shell . . . into the town. And still we live, with just sufficient spirit to jeer across our ramparts at our enemy."

Press report from
inside Mafeking

This painting, from the period, shows Londoners celebrating the relief of Mafeking in grand style. Pictures like this were the equivalent of modern television news.

Mafeking Night

After 217 interminable days, Mafeking was reached by a British relief column. Back in London, May 17, 1900, had been a normal spring day in the busy capital city. By 9:00 P.M. the day's work was over, but plenty of Londoners were still out and about. Evening papers were on sale at every street corner, and people scanned the headlines for news of the South African war — especially details of Baden-Powell's defense of Mafeking. Over the long months of siege, the little South African town, its brave citizens, and its cheeky, resourceful commanding officer had become familiar to readers.

The British people had taken Baden-Powell to their hearts. Mafeking had been more than a small South African town — it had become a symbol of the British Empire. The survival of the empire rested on Baden-Powell's resisting an army three times the size of the settlement.

Weeks before, Agnes Baden-Powell had written to her brother, "Everyone is talking of you. . . . [Y]our photo is in all the shops now . . . and they say yours is first favourite and sells best."

This evening, the evening of May 17, as always, Londoners hoped to hear that Mafeking's ordeal would soon be over.

Suddenly a whisper, then a murmur, then a great shout was heard: "Mafeking has been relieved!" Reuters International News Agency had flashed a message to the Fleet Street offices of the *Daily Telegraph*, and soon a poster outside the Mansion House, official residence of London's lord mayor, proclaimed the good news:

"MAFEKING HAS BEEN RELIEVED. FOOD HAS ENTERED THE GARRISON. ENEMY DISPERSED."

Hero of the hour

The normally staid British public went wild with joy. Complete strangers shook hands or embraced in the street. New reports interrupted performances of many shows. Everyone joined in cheering Baden-Powell and singing the British national anthem. London had never seen such a night of rejoicing.

B-P was the hero of the hour. "Three cheers for Baden-Powell!" was called out every few minutes. And so, with the successful end to the siege, fame came to Baden-Powell. He was just what the public needed: a modest hero with a sense of fun, and he rose to the occasion with dignity.

"Of course Baden-Powell had longed to be successful and had been tormented by ambition since childhood, but the scale of the fame thrust upon him by the editors and proprietors of the . . . press was beyond his comprehension. He was [only] a colonel, yet he had become as famous as the Commander-in-Chief and his Chief of Staff."
Tim Jeal, in his biography, Baden-Powell

Baden-Powell did not like the fame and adulation brought by events in Mafeking, calling it "damnable notoriety." But he knew he had to accept the fact that now he would always be a public figure — with the pressures and responsibilities which that involved.

He received thousands of letters, especially from young boys who had read about his exploits and wanted to ask his advice. Somehow they recognized that this famous soldier was not stuffy, but approachable and genuinely interested in their problems. B-P, as everyone now called him, was delighted by these letters. He replied carefully to each one, remembering the boys of Mafeking, those dreadful nuisances who had changed so quickly into brave and helpful members of the community.

Promoted to major general

In 1900, Baden-Powell was promoted to major general. At the age of forty-three, he was the youngest major general in the British army.

He stayed on in South Africa for nearly three years and during this time was responsible for the creation of the South African Constabulary, or police force. The force had its own uniform, designed by B-P, and members' training was of a much more individual nature than the usual army training. The constabulary soon became detached from the army, fulfilling its role not only as a military unit but also as a friendly source of help to communities.

Returning to England in the spring of 1903 to take up the post of inspector general of cavalry, Baden-Powell found many changes. He had left a country that had been at the peak of its prosperity, but the Boer War had taken its toll — trade was depressed, wages had dropped, and unemployment was rising. Many felt the loss of Queen Victoria, who had died in 1901 after a reign of 63 years.

One problem in particular worried Baden-Powell. Young people were turning to vandalism, drunkenness, and crime, and B-P despaired. He would see them, "thousands of boys and young men, pale, narrow-chested, hunched-up, miserable specimens, smoking endless cigarettes, numbers of them betting."

As Baden-Powell became a national hero, people flocked to buy Mafeking souvenirs. Badges, scarves, plates, and other articles were on sale, mostly bearing pictures of B-P complete with his famous hat. Baden-Powell disliked this publicity and adulation, but his reputation made people more willing to support his new Scouting movement.

Aids to Scouting becomes popular

B-P found that *Aids to Scouting*, the book he had written before the siege of Mafeking, was rapidly becoming a best-seller. Of course, his new status as a national hero had certainly boosted sales, but more important was the way in which his ideas on character and fitness training appealed to many readers outside the army.

The book outlined the ideas that Baden-Powell had put into practice as a colonel in India. It explained that courage, self-reliance, confidence, and judgment could be developed by training. But, most important, it described Baden-Powell's basic methods — dividing the men into small groups, making training enjoyable and entertaining, using various games and contests, and awarding badges for success and achievement.

Training boys for peace

Over the next two or three years, Baden-Powell gave much thought to the need for someone to help the boys he saw as he toured the country. He began to

"Loafers" and "Wasters," as B-P called them, were bored, often delinquent boys who roamed the streets smoking and getting into trouble. "Go into any . . . back alley where working lads congregate and hear what they talk about and think about, and you will come away ashamed at the results of our so-called civilization," he told a Scouting colleague. *"But it is not the fault of the boys"* — they were going wrong *"only for want of hands to guide them the right way towards being useful."* It was Scouting that could give them this guidance.

prepare the ideas for training young men that would become the Scout movement.

B-P read every book he could find on youth organizations. The one that interested him most was *The Birch-bark Roll of the Woodcraft Indians*, by Ernest Thompson Seton. Seton was a naturalist, an artist, and an expert on Indian lore and tradition.

Baden-Powell was impressed by Seton's use of woodcraft and tracking as educational leisure activities for young people. When the two men met and exchanged ideas, B-P felt he had gained some valuable insights.

The early books that Baden-Powell had written concentrated on training men for war; now he wanted to help the boys develop themselves for peace. Scouting was to be a means for young men to become better citizens by learning about themselves — their skills, their abilities, and their weaknesses — and by learning to cope with them. The emphasis of the movement was to be on doing something good and on improving the boys' character.

The idea grows

Baden-Powell's idea for a Scout organization was now taking shape, but he needed to get other people interested. To do so, he wrote two documents, *Boy Scouts, A Suggestion* and *Boy Scouts Scheme*. He was able to have them printed and circulated among some of his friends, and was pleased when he got an enthusiastic response from them. They urged him to develop his Scouting ideas further and to make a handbook available.

Having completed his term as inspector general of cavalry, Baden-Powell was promoted to lieutenant general in June 1907. He was then placed in the army's reserve. After thirty years, he no longer had any military responsibilities and was able to devote himself entirely to his new project.

Before starting to write his basic handbook, *Scouting for Boys*, however, he wanted to be sure that his ideas would work in practice.

To test his ideas and procedures, Baden-Powell organized a camp — the very first camp of the Scouting movement.

A treasured African souvenir, B-P's kudu horn roused the boys each morning at the Brownsea Island camp. Later the horn reveille was also a feature of the Scout training camps, the camp set up to produce suitable and well-qualified leaders for the new Scout troops.

The first Scouts

At the end of July 1907, twenty-two boys set out for Brownsea Island, a tiny island off the southern coast of Great Britain. They were an odd mixture — hard-working farm lads, privileged youths from private schools, boys from poor urban areas whose expenses were subsidized by well-wishers. Some were going with brothers or school friends; some perhaps felt slightly apprehensive. All wore smart, neat, and rather formal Sunday suits, but clutched bags or suitcases containing shorts and flannel shirts.

The main feeling was one of mounting excitement, for these boys had been specially invited to camp for a week with Lieutenant General Baden-Powell, the famous hero of Mafeking!

Baden-Powell had made meticulously careful preparations for this camp. Brownsea Island was the ideal spot — secluded yet not far from the mainland, with varied terrain and sandy beaches, and wood for fire and shelter. Tents, bedding, boats, cooking gear, and other items were found. B-P took great care over the selection of the boys. He wanted to be sure that they came from as many different social and economic backgrounds as possible.

Curlews, Ravens, Wolves, and Bulls

On the first morning of camp, Baden-Powell divided the boys into four patrols — Curlews, Ravens, Wolves, and Bulls. Each boy was given a shoulder knot of tape to show which patrol he belonged to: yellow for Curlews, red for Ravens, blue for Wolves, and green for Bulls. The patrol leaders also had a staff with an appropriate flag.

There were badges, too: for each boy, a brass fleur-de-lis (the symbol that Baden-Powell had used for his troops in India) and a brass scroll bearing the words "Be Prepared." This was to be earned by passing a few tests.

That night the boys gathered around a campfire. B-P told them stories from his army career and taught them the "Eengonyama" song, the Zulu chorus that had impressed him in Africa. The campfire and the stories told around it characterized the warm atmosphere of the camp.

"For thousands of boys who had never slept away from home, and for many more who had never left their home towns even for a day, this idea of going off with friends on an ambitious expedition was intoxicating."

Tim Jeal, in his biography, Baden-Powell

These boys in their baggy shorts and suspenders may not look much like today's smart Scouts, but the improvised uniforms were all part of the pioneering fun of the very first Scout camp on Brownsea Island. In this rare photograph of the camp, Robert Baden-Powell (also wearing a makeshift uniform) explains a game to some of the boys.

Modern Scouts step out to experience outdoor freedom and excitement, part of the same challenging world of adventure which attracted those first boys to Brownsea Island in 1907.

Each day's activities had a different theme, such as crafts, lifesaving, or observing signs in nature and the behavior of animals. Stories and examples the group discussed around the campfire were put into practice with demonstrations the next morning. In the afternoon, these lessons were backed up by contests and games.

Each night a different patrol would take a turn at night duty. The chosen patrol had to go to a pre-arranged spot, set up camp, light fires, cook supper, and keep watch for "enemies" — other patrol leaders and B-P himself! B-P was particularly interested in the overnight camps. They would show whether his patrol system worked.

Success

On the final day of the camp, Baden-Powell invited the boys' parents and various guests to a special display of all the new skills the boys had learned. The display involved games, contests, and demonstrations. It was organized and carried out entirely by the boys.

The next morning, August 9, the camp broke up and the boys went reluctantly home, leaving B-P to evaluate the week's success.

Perhaps he was most delighted with the results of the patrol system. As he wrote later, "the organization of dividing the boys into patrols of five, with a senior boy in each as patrol leader, was the secret of our success. Each patrol leader was given full responsibility for the behaviour of his patrol at all times, in camp and in the field. The patrol was the unit for work or play. . . .

"The boys," he continued, "were put on their honour to carry out orders. Responsibility, discipline, and competitive rivalry were thus at once established and a good standard of development was assured throughout the troop."

B-P's experiment had been a success.

The Scout promise

Now, at last, Baden-Powell felt confident enough to publicize his scheme. He organized an intensive lecture tour, giving forty lectures to twenty-five thousand men and boys, in thirty different towns within seven weeks.

Between lectures he was working on *Scouting for Boys* and, on January 15, 1908, the first of six parts went on sale; every two weeks, a new section appeared on bookstands. Copies of the booklet were quickly snapped up. Boys and girls all over the country wanted to know what Lieutenant General Baden-Powell had to say.

The first booklet was made up of a number of features, stories, and games and also explained how to become a Scout.

Other articles outlined the ideals behind Scouting. Each boy who wanted to join would take the Scout Oath and would promise three things:

1. to be loyal to God and the king;
2. to help other people at all times; and
3. to obey the Scout Law.

The task of constructing a wigwam has this group of Scouts figuring out the best way to erect a wooden frame. Just as the very first Scouts learned new skills through friendly group activities, today boys and girls all over the world work together to solve problems and build confidence.

Above: In the well-known salute, the three fingers represent the three parts of the Scout Oath.

Below: An early Boy Scout helps a woman across a dangerous London street.

These three rules still form the essence of Scouting today, except that the first rule has been broadened to fit Scouts of all faiths from across the world.

The Scout uniform was also defined at this early stage. It included several reminders of B-P's army experiences: the broad-brimmed hat that he had adopted in Africa, the fleur-de-lis badge from India, plus the neckerchief and flannel shirt from his days in the bush. He also included the stick or "stave" that he had seen used by a fellow officer in the jungle to jump streams, test footings, and measure distances. The shorts and shoulder knots had been pioneered at the Brownsea Island camp.

Scouting for Boys listed five tests for new Scouts — tying knots, tracking, covering a mile (1.6 km) at "Scout's pace," knowing the Scout Law and signs, and learning how to fly the national flag properly. First Class Scouts had to pass seven further tests. To encourage the boys to reach a good standard, badges were awarded to them for passing the tests.

The idea catches on

In April 1908, *Scouting for Boys* was joined by a weekly magazine, *The Scout*. Packed with information, adventure stories, and suggestions for games and activities, *The Scout* reached a circulation of 110 thousand during its first year.

All over Britain, boys used broomsticks for staves, persuaded their mothers to shorten their pants, saved up for broad-brimmed hats, and set off to build campfires. They learned how to track and explored any available countryside — even if it was only the local park.

Older brothers, teachers, and Sunday school teachers were persuaded to become Scout instructors. They, too, studied *Scouting for Boys* in a desperate attempt to keep one jump ahead of their patrols.

Troops were formed all over Great Britain — in stately homes and in the slums, where few boys had boots and the uniform consisted of a thick stick, a schoolbag, a haversack, or kind of backpack, and — for the really lucky ones — a belt with a coil of rope hanging from it. Every pioneer Scout troop had its own story.

In the summer of 1908, there was a second camp. The thirty Scouts who participated had won their places through a competition organized by *The Scout*. Baden-Powell would have liked every Scout in the land to be there, but by now there were far too many.

Camps were to become a central part of the Scouting movement, and more and more were organized. Some of the early camps were extremely large, with up to two hundred Scouts taking part. While B-P felt that such large numbers hindered the real benefits of Scout camp, such as close contact with nature and individual friendship between boys and leaders, they were necessary because of the shortage of equipment and instructors.

Following the success of the first competition in 1908, *The Scout* ran a similar one in 1909. The prize was two weeks at B-P's camp, with places for one hundred boys. The boys were split into two groups of fifty and each group spent one week on land and one week aboard the training ship *Mercury*. It was the success of this "sea camp" that led to the official beginning of the Sea Scouts in 1910.

Baden-Powell was surprised by the sudden growth

"Nothing should ever escape the eye of a scout; he should have eyes at the back of his head; he should . . . [notice] little trifles or distant objects that have not struck the attention of his comrades. Always notice all peculiar features and landmarks while going over strange ground . . . so that you may be able to find your way back again by them."
Robert Baden-Powell,
in Reconnaissance
and Scouting

Baden-Powell telling a yarn around the campfire. His eccentricities added something special to Scouting, making it more successful than other youth movements.

The Scouts' Evening Meal — NOT as Mother makes it.

The Sleuth Hounds — Boy Scouts tracing a Desperado (after the manner of the Native Trackers).

of Scouting in 1908 and 1909. The secret of his success was that in 1908 there were few organized leisure activities for boys and Scouting filled a gap. Its informal approach and young, friendly leaders were a refreshing change in those days of strict parents, teachers, and clergy.

But the reasons for the enduring appeal of Scouting go deeper than this. Children have always enjoyed playing outdoor games, testing their skills and abilities as they grow older, and joining with other young people in gangs or secret societies. At camp they could learn to stalk and track, to cook on an open fire, to put up tents and make shelters, to make a mattress from ferns, to be independent yet part of a team. For the early Scouts the uniform and the badges all reinforced this sense of belonging.

Secrets of success

Perhaps for the first time, they made decisions for themselves, either as patrol members or in the larger democratic setting of the troop. And without pressure from parents or other adults, they accepted the commitment of the Scout Oath and the self-discipline of the Scout Law.

All these elements were (and still are) found in Scouting. But, of course, in those days, there was the extra ingredient of B-P's personality. Humorous and unpredictable, the optimistic B-P was also a man of high ideals. Over the years the inspirational side of Scouting has continued to attract the idealism of young people. It continues to offer them a practical opportunity to build a better world for the future.

So many boys were determined to become Scouts that the very popularity of Scouting brought its own problems. Some boys were going out in the countryside unsupervised while others were in the care of self-appointed Scoutmasters who were unsuitable for the job. Baden-Powell was determined not to cramp initiative, but he admitted that local committees were necessary to oversee Scouting in each area.

Clearly the movement needed a central organization. The first moves toward achieving this were made in 1909 and 1910.

Opposite: Part of a series of postcards popular at the time, these two cartoons poke affectionate fun at the adventures and misadventures of the early Scouts. After sampling his friend's cooking, one unfortunate Scout looks quite ill, while the dog wisely refuses to eat an uneaten portion. The lower postcard shows a brave troop on a tracking exercise about to be surprised by a burglar or "desperado" they are tracking.

"Far from seeming a strait-jacket of rules, Baden-Powell's scheme offered freedom far beyond anything most of [the boys] had ever encountered."
Tim Jeal, in his biography, Baden-Powell

"Like members of an early Christian sect the first Boy Scouts were subjected to frequent ridicule. . . . But ridicule seemed a small price to pay for this organized escape from 'repressive schoolmasters, moralizing parsons and coddling parents.' There was no radio then, no cinema, far too few playing fields and most schools were tyrannical places. Scouting seemed heaven-sent to boys and to those who cared about them."
Tim Jeal, in his biography, Baden-Powell

The Crystal Palace rally

For the Scouts themselves, the high point of these early years was the Scout rally of 1909. Despite pouring rain, eleven thousand Scouts turned up at London's spacious Crystal Palace on September 4 to demonstrate their skills and to listen to an address from Baden-Powell. Mounting the platform, he was greeted by a roar of welcome and thousands of Scout hats being twirled on upraised poles.

Silence fell as he read out a telegram from King Edward VII, sending the Scouts congratulations and good wishes. This created a sense of excitement and marked the beginning of a long association between Scouting and the British royal family.

The success of the Crystal Palace rally meant that Scouting had really arrived. Nothing was going to stop it now, even though the movement had its critics. Some people thought Scouting too militaristic while others, in complete contrast, wanted to ally it with more nationalistic youth groups.

The Girl Guides

As part of the Crystal Palace rally, Baden-Powell mingled with the Scouts, chatting and joking. Suddenly, among the thousands of boys, he noticed a small group of girls. He could see that they were wearing a version of the Scout uniform — and determined expressions.

"Who are you?" asked the astonished B-P.

Girls, during this period, were expected to behave in a ladylike manner, look after the home, and take second place to their brothers. For girls to want to join the Scouts was a shock not only to B-P but to the rest of society as well. The girls were determined, and with their homemade uniforms and knapsacks they had taken part in all the activities that the boys had. They wanted to be a part of the movement.

Things were just beginning to change, but not fast enough for many girls, including the determined band who wanted to become Scouts. These girls recalled the opposition they had met every step of the way. It had taken real courage to go to the Crystal Palace rally and to face the great Lieutenant General Baden-Powell on that September day in 1909.

A determined "Girl Scout" (the original British Girl Guides had not yet formed a separate organization) makes her presence felt at the Crystal Palace rally in 1909. Hedged in by petty restrictions, the average girl of the day welcomed the chance to shorten her skirts and join in outdoor activities with other young people. Under B-P's sister Agnes, and later under his young wife Olave, the Girl Guides offered girls a chance to take their place as responsible members of the community.

These pioneers made Baden-Powell realize that girls must not be left out of the Scouting movement. At this time B-P was not married and, apart from his mother and sister, he was not really close to any women. His life as a soldier had been spent with other men, and he had given very little thought to young girls and their education, although he had realized it was necessary to include them in the movement. By November 1910, more than six thousand girls — on their own initiative — had written to register themselves as Scouts. They could not be ignored.

B-P turned to his sister for support. Agnes wanted to help. She was a keen naturalist, a successful bee-keeper, and talented at all kinds of handicrafts. Eagerly she directed her energies into organizing the girls into a movement of their own under the name of the Girl Guides, called the Girl Scouts in some other nations, including the United States.

B-P's decision

Baden-Powell's decision to give the Guides a separate organization with activities of their own has sometimes been questioned. In 1909, many parents were concerned about the growing agitation for

"I have had several . . . letters from little girls asking me if they may share the delights of Scouting life with the boys. But of course they may! I am always glad of girls' patrols being formed."
Robert Baden-Powell

After 1914, younger boys joined the Cub Scouts. Baden-Powell used ideas from Rudyard Kipling's famous Jungle Book *in selecting Cub Scout activities. Here an early pack joins in a Grand Howl. Notice that the two helpers are both women; at a time when many women were expected to remain at home, the Scouting movement offered them useful and satisfying activities.*

women's rights. Many of the older generation disapproved of this agitation. They were not ready to see their daughters sharing activities with numbers of boys. Because of B-P's decision to have separate organizations, the girls' parents accepted Guiding. The organization quietly trained resourceful women who were eager to take their place in the community when attitudes finally changed — although the two organizations remain separate.

Guiding made a rather slow start in Britain. By 1916, there were still four times as many Scouts as there were Guides. Some of the first girls in Scouting were not too pleased when they were transformed into "Guides" and offered such activities as cooking, nursing, and homemaking. Their troop names were also changed from exciting names of animals to those of flowers! Only during the 1920s did Britain's Girl Guides movement come into its own.

Scouting developments worldwide

Meanwhile boys flocked to join the Scouts. The first census in 1910 recorded a membership of well over 100 thousand, with nearly eight thousand Scoutmasters, who were beginning to get together for special training and discussion.

Scouting was becoming an international movement. *Scouting for Boys* had become a best seller and was widely translated. Soon Scout troops were started in Australia, Canada, New Zealand, South Africa, Chile, India, British Guiana (now Guyana), Ceylon (now Sri Lanka), Jamaica, Rhodesia (now Zimbabwe), Singapore, Denmark, Finland, France, Greece, Russia (now the Soviet Union), and Holland.

At least seventy more countries were added to the roll; within twenty years, there were approximately two million Scouts. There were Scouts, Girl Scouts, and Girl Guides in every corner of the world.

In London a helpful Scout guided an American tourist lost in a thick fog back to his hotel but refused a tip for his services. The visitor, a publisher named William Boyce, was so impressed that in 1910 he started the first American Scout troop.

Years later that nameless London boy would be remembered as "the unknown Scout whose

At mischief before joining. Boy Scouts' good use of Holiday Hours.

"Be Prepared" (Swinstead 1916)

faithfulness in the performance of the daily good turn brought the Scout movement to the United States of America."

Sir Robert

Shortly after the Crystal Palace rally, King Edward VII made Baden-Powell *Sir* Robert Baden-Powell. B-P described the ceremony as "very embarrassing — and very jolly." He kept forgetting his title: "I didn't realize at first who they were alluding to when they said 'Sir Robert' does this or that."

Officially Baden-Powell was still in the British army. But now Scouting was taking up much of his time and energy. In May 1910, he resigned at the suggestion of King Edward VII, who believed Baden-Powell was providing a greater service as a leader of the Scouts than he possibly could as a soldier. It was a major step. B-P had been a soldier for most of his life and now, at the age of fifty-three, he was on the threshold of a second career.

The first two years of Sir Robert's full-time commitment to Scouting passed in a whirl of activity. He visited Canada, the United States, Scandinavia, Holland, and Belgium. At home he supervised the growth of Scout headquarters, ran a Scoutmasters' training course, and organized Scout participation in the coronation of King George V in 1911.

Olave

By January 1912, Baden-Powell was on board the SS *Arcadian*, bound for a lecture tour of the United States. As he enjoyed the fresh air on deck, he noticed a figure that seemed vaguely familiar. He searched his memory and relived a London morning some two years before.

Hurrying to Knightsbridge Barracks he had noticed a young woman exercising her spaniel in London's Hyde Park. What had struck him was the purposeful grace of her quick, determined movements. That girl, thought B-P, must "be possessed of honesty of purpose and common sense as well as a spirit of adventure."

He had forgotten all about her, but now here she was on the *Arcadian*.

Dark-haired Olave Soames was twenty when Robert Baden-Powell first noticed her walking her dog in London's Hyde Park, but he did not actually meet his future wife until nearly three years later. Olave (pronounced "OH-lev," the name is a female form of the Danish Olaf) loved sports, travel, and the outdoor life. She had a cheerful personality, and entered enthusiastically into all of B-P's projects.

Olave Soames with a young Scout. She was associated with Scouting as soon as her engagement to B-P was announced. Although she was a little shy at first, she soon gained confidence and within a year was delighting large audiences with her charm and common sense.

A shipboard romance

Miss Olave St. Clair Soames was delighted to be introduced to the legendary Robert Baden-Powell. During the voyage they talked constantly. They discovered that they had much in common — including a joint birthday on February 22. This date would later be set aside as the Guides' "Thinking Day." By the time the ship docked in Kingston, Jamaica, where Olave was going ashore, the pair had grown very close.

Olave Soames could see no reason to put off their marriage, but Baden-Powell was still helping to support his mother and sister. He was, at the time, worried about his finances — although this concern was unnecessary.

The difference in their ages could also have been a problem, because Baden-Powell was fifty-five while Olave was only twenty-three. But B-P never lost his active ways and his unpredictable sense of fun. It seemed Olave almost worshipped him, sharing his interests fully.

"My future bride is as keen about scouting as I am. She will help me in the work, so that my marriage instead of taking me from the movement will bring in another assistant to it, and one who loves the Scouts as they, I am sure, will love her so soon as they get to know her."

Robert Baden-Powell, in
The Scout, *1912*

Heather Baden-Powell shoulders her Teddy bear in this painting by her proud father. B-P was a devoted father and entertained his three young children with an endless store of jokes, stories, and rhymes. He encouraged games and rearranged the furniture so that Peter, Heather, and Betty could climb around the house without touching the floor. As she grew up, Heather was especially close to her father, sharing his interest in riding and painting.

A life's partner

Baden-Powell continued his journey, visiting the United States, Japan, China, New Guinea, Australia, and New Zealand before returning home by way of South Africa in September 1912.

After a meeting with Olave's father, he wrote this letter to his mother:

"Dearest Mother,

"I have been wondering what to give you as a birthday present, but I think I've got one now that will please you (as I hope and believe) — and that is a daughter-in-law for you!

"Olave Soames whom I met on board the *Arcadian* travelling with her father promises to be a very good one. I hope you will like her half as much as I do.

"She has only one fault (and both George and Frank told me that in getting a wife you must overlook a fault or two if she is on the whole what you want). Her fault is that she is young, but she has an old head on her shoulders and is clever and wise and very bright and cheery. . . .

"So I came here . . . last night to dine and sleep, and to have a talk with her father. . . . I must tell you all about it when I get home on Monday — and get your consent and good wishes."

Marriage

So Lieutenant General Sir Robert Baden-Powell and Olave St. Clair Soames were married quietly on October 30, 1912. They spent a late honeymoon camping in Algeria. This was something of a test for Olave, as she had never camped before, but she passed with distinction.

"I am built for camp as my beloved is!" she recorded in her diary, while Robert wrote to his mother, "Olave is a perfect wonder in camp — thoroughly enjoys the life and is as good as a backwoodsman at it. She is a splendid walker, a good scout — never loses her way . . . and she looks after me like a mother, absolutely spoils me." Robert had found in Olave the mixture of fun, tomboyishness, and sensitivity he had been searching for.

When the B-Ps, as everyone called them, returned home, the Scouts gave them a wedding present. A hundred thousand Scouts had contributed a penny each to buy them a motorcar painted in the Scouts' dark green with yellow trim, complete with the Scout badge and motto.

Universal changes

Between 1914 and 1918 the turmoil of World War I caused great changes. Many Scouts and Girl Guides, like everyone else, would lose their homes and lives. Despite war, the number of young people in Scouting and Scoutmasters worldwide rose by forty-one thousand — from 152,333 to 193,731.

Meanwhile, three children were born to the B-Ps: Peter was born on his parents' first wedding anniversary; Heather was born on June 1, 1915; and Betty was born on April 16, 1917.

Mynthurst, the family home until 1919, as painted by Baden-Powell. He found true happiness at home with his wife and children. At home life was full of painting, writing, and comedy. It took all the energy that B-P possessed to achieve all these things, as well as to pioneer and run the Scouting movement.

On January 29, 1919, the family moved into the house which was to be their home for the next twenty years. It was in the village of Bentley, in Hampshire, a county in south central England. Soon the B-Ps were part of the local community. Baden-Powell designed a village sign, which still stands at the end of the lane leading to Pax (Peace) Hill — as Olave named their house to celebrate the end of the war.

A time of change

After the war, the Scouting movement faced many problems. One important one was the challenge of establishing the right activities to capture the enthusiasm of the various age groups. There were no problems with the younger boys — the problems lay with the fourteen- to eighteen-year-olds.

To keep the older boys interested, Baden-Powell worked out a new range of activities for them and gave them their own title of "Senior Scouts." A year later, this was changed to "Rover Scouts."

Perhaps the greatest changes, though, were happening in Guiding. During the four years of World War I, women had kept Great Britain running. While the men were away fighting, wives and daughters proved that women could handle many difficult jobs. Votes for women became a reality in the postwar period. The Guides were ready to take their place in this new world.

Olave takes the lead

Restricting girls to domestic skills was beginning to look old-fashioned, so B-P realized the group needed a major reorganization. In February 1918, he published *Girl Guiding*, which described the British movement's new look for girls. They were encouraged to enjoy more outside activities — observing nature and learning outdoor skills.

Olave Baden-Powell, young, energetic, and committed to Robert's ideals, was able to inspire a new generation of girls. There was a rush to join. Within three months, numbers had tripled. By 1932, there would be almost 500 thousand Guides in Britain. By 1975, there were more than six-and-a-half million Girl Guides and Girl Scouts worldwide.

Baden-Powell encouraged Olave to take the lead, so in 1918, at the age of twenty-nine, Olave Baden-Powell became chief Guide. In 1930, her title was changed to "World Chief Guide." More formally, until B-P's death in 1941, she was known as Lady Baden-Powell. As is traditional, after his death, she became known as Olave Lady Baden-Powell.

Jamboree!

The Scouting movement had survived the war and was now stronger than ever. By 1920, it had almost a quarter of a million members. Public attitudes were changing — Scouts were now admired and respected.

It was time for B-P to stage an event that would bring the Scouts together and focus public attention on their achievements. This event, scheduled for the summer of 1920, was to be more than a rally or an exhibition. He would call it a jamboree.

"What did it mean?" asked his friends. B-P looked it up in a dictionary: "JAMBOREE: A carousal; a noisy drinking bout; a spree; any noisy merrymaking." Not very dignified, but B-P stuck to his word and a Scout jamboree was advertised for the first week in August 1920 at London's Olympia, a huge glass-roofed exhibition hall.

Baden-Powell had just appointed an international commissioner, who sent invitations to Scouts all over the world. Acceptances flooded back — ranging from large American and Dutch contingents (four hundred from Holland) to four from Siam (now Thailand) and just two Scouts from Japan.

By the end of July, eight thousand Scouts from twenty-one countries and twelve British dependencies had converged on London. For eight days, huge audiences admired the skill with which the hall was transformed into island, mountain, and jungle scenes as the Scouts presented a series of team displays, contests, pageants, and concerts.

A special show was planned for the closing night of the jamboree. The following morning, the Scouts would have to say good-bye to the new friends they had made and set off on their homeward journeys. But first, there was a very special surprise for Baden-Powell — planned by the Scouts!

Olave Baden-Powell had a flair for organization and boundless enthusiasm. Later, these carried her through daunting amounts of paperwork and official duties as chief commissioner and "World Chief Guide."

Chief Scout of the world

Above: The "Five Fingers, One Hand" grouping at a jamboree symbolizes international bonding. Opposite, from bottom: Badges mark the success of Scouting: Brunei (Scouting since 1951), Dominica (since 1929), Cyprus (since 1914), and New Zealand (since 1908).

As the Scouts paraded with their national flags at the climax of the closing ceremony on August 7, B-P was amazed to hear a voice ring out: "We, the Scouts of the world, salute you, Sir Robert Baden-Powell — Chief Scout of the World!"

For a moment he hesitated before stepping forward to address the suddenly silent crowd. "Brother Scouts," he said, "I ask you to make a

solemn choice. Differences exist between the peoples of the world in thought and sentiment, just as they do in language and physique. The war has taught us that if one nation tries to impose its particular will on others, cruel reaction is bound to follow. The jamboree has taught us that if we exercise mutual forbearance and give and take, then there is sympathy and harmony.

"If it be your will, let us go forth from here

determined that we will develop among ourselves and our boys that comradeship, through the worldwide spirit of the Scout brotherhood, so that we may help to develop peace and happiness in the world and good will among men. Brother Scouts, answer me — will you join me in this endeavor?"

Baden-Powell, who had spent so many years as a soldier trained in the arts of war, was delivering a moving appeal for peace and international cooperation. Without any hesitation, the Scouts answered his question with a resounding "YES!"

Lord Baden-Powell of Gilwell

Acclaimed as chief Scout of the world, Baden-Powell might well have settled down to a quieter life with his young family. Now sixty-three years old, and beginning to feel the effects of the illnesses and wounds of his army years, he remained as active as ever, always up at 5:00 A.M. to be sure he could achieve all the tasks he set for himself.

With Pax Hill as his base, and Olave as his constant companion, he journeyed thousands of miles to visit Scouts in India, Scandinavia, North America, and South Africa.

International jamborees now became regular events. The third one, scheduled for 1929, was to be a special celebration of twenty-one years of Scouting. From the small group of boys that had attended the first camp on Brownsea Island, Scouting had now grown into a thriving international movement with a membership of nearly two million.

At the jamboree, there was to be a presentation to B-P, so Lady B-P was asked to find out what he would like. After much thought, Baden-Powell could suggest only a pair of new suspenders. A grinning party of Irish Scouts did give him some splendid green ones, but he also received a check, a portrait of himself, and a Rolls-Royce car with a camper attached. He was rather less delighted with being offered a peerage, or status of nobility. He would have preferred to remain plain B-P. But realizing that the award was really intended for the whole Scouting movement, he agreed to become Lord Baden-Powell of Gilwell.

The peacemaker

As Baden-Powell's daughter Heather later wrote, "This should have been the culmination of my father's life work. But far from it! Although now aged seventy-two, he and my mother (a mere forty), within the space of the next nine years, completed two world tours, a tour of Africa and then of India, not to mention lesser trips on the continent, . . . Jamborees in Hungary and Holland and three . . . cruises with ships full of Scouters and Guiders."

An important aspect of Baden-Powell's work might be described as troubleshooting. He ensured cooperation between Protestant and Roman Catholic Canadians, and he had seen "a united band of brother Scouts" overcoming racial barriers in an India yearning for the end of British rule.

Baden-Powell was particularly anxious about South Africa. He was saddened to realize that, in the land he loved best after Britain, racial prejudice was making a mockery of the basic principles of Scouting. Attending a Scout conference in Durban, he fought

"I am the richest man in the world for I believe that the richest man is not the man who has the most money but the man who has fewer wants."
B-P, on being asked what he wanted to mark Scouting's twenty-first anniversary

"It has given me great pleasure to mark this signal event in your history by conferring a peerage on the Chief Scout. Ever since its inception he has been the mainspring of this great adventure, from its small and almost humble beginning until today, when you number nearly two million in your ranks. The recognition of his valuable services to the cause will be welcomed by all who realize the importance of training the world's youth both in mind and body."
King George V, 1929

"Roses, sunshine and peace" was a visitor's description of the garden at Pax Hill, the country home where the Baden-Powell family could relax, far away from the pressures of big occasions and official appearances. Busy as he was, Baden-Powell always found time for his home and family, and for activities in the local village community.

for the integration of black, white, and Asian Scouts within the movement. He was not happy with the final decision to run separate branches with a central council, especially because white extremists refused to join even this.

In the years that followed, the Boy Scouts Association of South Africa stuck to the spirit of Scouting in a troubled situation, struggling to run interracial activities and sending black representatives to international gatherings.

Scouting banned

In Germany and Italy the movement had got off to an early start but Scouting was having problems with the governments of the day.

Scouting came to Germany in 1909, when *Scouting for Boys* was translated into German. For years, it was one of the most popular of the various German youth organizations.

But in 1933, Germany's new Nazi leader, Adolf Hitler, ordered the national youth leader to abolish all youth groups except one: the *Hitler-Jugend*, or Hitler Youth. The German government made great efforts to encourage exchange visits and general cooperation between the Hitler Youth and British Scouting. So Baden-Powell visited the German embassy in London for discussions. He came away deeply concerned.

He believed that the totalitarian Nazi government had taken key elements of Scouting — such as hiking, camping, group loyalty, and national pride — and perverted them so they were used to persuade young people to accept Nazi ideas such as racial intolerance. But surely, severing all connection with the young Germans would only make things worse.

Ultimately the Boy Scouts Association in Great Britain kept aloof from the Hitler Youth, while in Germany the true principles of Scouting were not forgotten. The Scouts went underground and re-emerged after World War II ended in 1945.

Much the same story unfolded in Italy. This country had been a charter member of the world Scout movement, with the first troops formed in 1912. But the flourishing movement was banned in 1927 by Italy's Fascist leader, Benito Mussolini. He tried to

replace it with his own militant youth organizations, the Balilla, which was for young boys, and the Avanguardisti, for teenage boys.

B-P went to Italy and argued with Mussolini, who told him that he should be flattered — the Balilla was an improvement on Scouting. Undaunted, B-P attacked the Balilla because of the pressure to join, the emphasis on national superiority, and its failure to encourage spiritual ideals or individual development.

Mussolini's ban was not lifted. Yet in Italy too, the spirit of Scouting lived on, as fathers and older brothers hid their uniforms to pass on to a new generation of Scouts when better times came.

South African Scouts set an example of racial harmony in true Baden-Powell tradition. All Scouts and Guides in this troubled country have fought long and hard against the country's laws in order to have fully integrated troops.

B-P's last jamboree

The world chief Scout seemed tireless, so it shocked everyone when serious illness struck Baden-Powell early in 1933. He had a dangerous operation and nearly died, but at seventy-seven he was still able to fight back. In 1935, 1936, and 1937, he and Olave

Baden-Powell toured Australia, Canada, South Africa, and India.

But at last a note of farewell began to appear in many of Baden-Powell's speeches, and he seemed to know instinctively that the Fifth World Jamboree of 1937 would be his last one.

Holland hosted this gathering of thirty thousand Scouts from more than thirty countries. As Heather Baden-Powell explains, "The whole atmosphere was just as my father intended it to be — a happy crowd of youngsters gathered together to make friends and understand one another."

On the final day B-P watched a spectacular march as flag after flag was displayed by Scouts clad in a rich variety of national costumes. Each group was proud of its own culture and traditions, but the friendships formed at the jamboree — like the spirit of Scouting itself — knew no boundaries of race, nationality, or background.

"Now good-bye"

B-P's theatrical talents always came to his aid on big occasions. Old and frail as he was, he held the vast crowd in breathlessly silent attention. He had never been a large or physically imposing man. At eighty,

On a visit to Paris, Baden-Powell was welcomed by enthusiastic French Scouts brandishing their hats high on their Scout staffs. During the 1920s and 1930s, Robert and Olave Baden-Powell journeyed thousands of miles, both to rally support for Scouting and Guiding and to solve problems; in these years before World War II, B-P knew the movement must join the quest for peace.

the figure in the familiar Scout uniform looked small and fragile. Yet his voice rang out clear and strong, just as it had on the parade grounds of India, in the town square at Mafeking, and at the jamborees of 1920 and 1929.

"The time has come for me to say good-bye. You know that many of us will never meet again in this world. I am in my eighty-first year and am nearing the end of my life. Most of you are at the beginning, and I want your lives to be happy and successful. You can make them so by doing your best to carry out the Scout Law all your days, whatever your station and whoever you are.

"I want you all to preserve the badge of the jamboree on your uniform. . . . It will be a reminder of the happy times you have had here in camp; it will remind you to take the . . . points of the Scout Law as your guide in life; and it will remind you of the many friends to whom you have held out the hand of friendship and so helped through goodwill to bring about God's reign of peace among men. Now good-bye. God bless you all!"

A silver wedding anniversary present

On October 30, 1937, Olave and B-P celebrated twenty-five years of marriage. Among the many wedding anniversary presents they received was a check made up of contributions from Boy Scouts, Girl Scouts, Girl Guides, Cubs, and Brownies everywhere.

With this money, the B-Ps moved to Nyeri, near Mount Kenya, in Africa. It was here that Baden-Powell spent his last years. They named the house Paxtu, partially as a version of "Pax, too" and "Pax, two" in memory of their Hampshire home, but mostly because *Paxtu* means "complete" in Swahili.

For the first time in their married life, they were alone. "We are utterly and supremely happy here," Olave wrote, "and almost every other minute we keep saying to each other how heavenly it is and how lucky we are to be here."

At last Baden-Powell had to slow down, but he could not be idle. With more leisure he was able to spend time writing and drawing, and produced enough articles and paintings to fill three books.

On a "Visit of the Chiefs," Olave and B-P would stay at rallies for an hour, make a five-minute speech, and move on to the next welcoming committee, asking that they not be presented with bouquets or souvenirs!

Above and right: From the very first, camping has been one of the most attractive aspects of Scouting. It is as popular today as it was back in 1907, when B-P took the boys to Brownsea Island. For many young people it is their first stay away from home. Campers learn independence in challenging new surroundings and develop strong bonds of friendship.

Gone home

But B-P was gradually growing weaker. He was not ill, just old and very tired. He died at Paxtu on January 8, 1941, just weeks before his eighty-fourth birthday. He had always declined the offer of a grave in London's Westminster Abbey, and according to his own wishes, was buried in the little cemetery at Nyeri, with full military procedures and an attendant guard of Scouts. His simple gravestone bears his name and the Scout trail sign for "gone home."

The title of "Chief Scout of the World" died with him. There have been many popular Scout leaders since then, but never another Baden-Powell. With characteristic thoroughness, Baden-Powell had left written messages of thanks and farewell to the Boy Scouts, Girl Scouts, Girl Guides, group leaders, and the general public.

Above, top: Friendships forged at camp can be something special. As B-P said at a South African camp in 1936, "I want to urge you to all make friends now among yourselves so that you will still be friends when you grow up and thus make a united team for your country."

Above, bottom: Jamboree: "A noisy party; a spree; any noisy merrymaking"; and judging from this 1975 jamboree, an unforgettable experience for the participants!

55

"Brother Scouts, I shall not pass this way again, but I want all of you gathered here to remember this night, and as you go your ways in the world, your job is to spread and keep alive this spirit of Brotherhood, and by doing so to help to bring about Peace and Goodwill on Earth."

B-P, speaking at a camp
in Australia, 1934

"The real way to get happiness is by giving out happiness to other people."

Baden-Powell's farewell
message to the Scouts,
quoted in Laszlo Nagy's
250 Million Scouts

In his final message to the Scouts, B-P urged them to "get happiness . . . by giving out happiness to other people" and "to try to leave this world a little better than you found it."

A sad homecoming

After B-P's death, Olave Baden-Powell tried to bury her personal despair in work for Kenyan women, when a letter from war-torn London persuaded her to return to Great Britain. In 1939, World War II had broken out. The editor of *The Guider* magazine wrote to Olave asking her to "come home and see for yourself what the Guides are doing in the war; you will never forgive yourself if you don't."

So Olave Baden-Powell left Paxtu and its memories for an unfamiliar wartime London of air raids and strict food rationing. Hampton Court, near London, was her base for the next thirty-one years; she spent only a limited amount of time in Britain, notching up 487 thousand miles (784,000 km) of air travel and more by sea, road, and rail.

As a living link with B-P and his ideals, Olave Baden-Powell encouraged the Scouts and Guides to try to heal the scars of World War II. Immediately after peace was declared in 1945, she visited France, Luxembourg, and Italy. One person she met was Robert Schaffner, the future prime minister of Luxembourg. He told her how the spirit of Scouting had given him the inner strength to survive the horrors of a concentration camp.

Scouting began to revive in countries where it had been banned. In Austria and Germany, units reappeared as if by magic. In Italy, too, the movement soon returned. At the Seventh World Jamboree, held in Austria in 1951, Italian, Japanese, and especially the German contingents were given an enthusiastic welcome back into international Scout gatherings.

Working for a better world

After the war, there was a dramatic increase in membership of the Scouting movement. From 1948 to 1950, the number of young people involved rose by nearly two million — from 3,306,000 to 5,160,147.

More than half of them were in the United States.

Ever since the early days of 1910, the Boy Scouts of America had been developing in their own way under the leadership of James E. West, a lawyer and campaigner for children's rights.

Laszlo Nagy, secretary general of the World Scout Bureau, has said that they were the first in the world to prove that "a youth movement born overseas, rooted in other traditions and subject to other requirements, can still be transplanted without losing or betraying its original spirit, ideas and principles."

In 1957, the centennial of B-P's birth was celebrated in a world that was being transformed by technology, by high-speed travel, and by the presence of mass communication.

In the West, the 1960s was a time when many young people examined traditional views handed down from their parents and grandparents. Suddenly they had more money and more leisure time — and more ways in which to spend them. Cheaper air travel opened up the world, and television brought news and pictures from India and Africa into Western homes. Baden-Powell's deepest convictions about the need for worldwide bonds of friendship and about his work for peace now seemed even more relevant than during his lifetime.

Young people realized, perhaps for the first time, that unfair distribution of the Earth's resources meant prosperity and materialism in the West and hunger and disease in the Third World. And the Earth's resources were not limitless. Unless mismanagement and pollution could be checked, the future was bleak for all the world's inhabitants.

Truly international

Over the years, Scout leaders realized that the organization needed updating. When its founder had been alive, the Girl Scouts, Girl Guides, and Boy Scouts had been under the ruling control of Baden-Powell. B-P believed that the decisions had to come from him alone — and the growth of the movement away from this was a gradual and difficult one.

Some older members were concerned that Baden-Powell's ideals would be forgotten or changed beyond recognition. But Olave spoke out for renewal. "Hats

The Boy Scouts, Girl Scouts, and Girl Guides have become truly international and the movement is growing more rapidly than ever before.

off to the past and sleeves up to the future" was her motto. She did not want a rigid, out-of-date system; more valuable would be a Scouting movement that could adapt to the times. The main need now was for a more truly international approach.

To deal with the spread of world Scouting, the Boy Scouts International Bureau came into being on October 11, 1920, based in London. To prevent the movement from becoming too insular, the bureau moved to Ottawa, Canada, on January 1, 1958, and finally to Geneva, Switzerland, on May 1, 1968. It is now called the World Scout Bureau.

In July 1959, the first World Jamboree held in the Third World took place in the Philippines. Twelve thousand boys from forty-four countries took part.

That same year, the first international Scouting conference to be held outside a Western country also took place in New Delhi, India. Among the many

people who attended the conference was India's prime minister, Pandit Nehru.

Over the years, leadership has also become more international. In 1931, a man from Japan was elected to the governing committee. In 1951, the first Arab was elected, and ten years later, in 1961, the first African took his seat on the committee.

Modern concerns

From the 1970s on, ecologists have worked to make people aware of the fragile balance of life on Earth. Respect for nature was nothing new for the Scouts. Deep awareness of the natural world had been part of B-P's character since those early days in the Copse. Scouts in many countries now clear trails, protect nature reserves, plant trees, make nests, and raise money for conservation work.

Olave lived to see and welcome all these

Above, left: From cooking, lighting fires, and building shelters to orienteering (a contest involving map-reading skills), outdoor adventure skills appeal to modern young people.

Above, right: You don't need to use a bridge to get across a river! Moments like this are at the heart of Scouting, as perhaps Baden-Powell realized when he wrote, "What a fine thing it would be to teach boys Scouting — tracking, woodcraft, life in the open, campfires, living in the backwoods."

59

developments, whether major reorganizations or smaller changes like the adoption of a new name, the "World Organization of the Scout Movement."

By the time Olave died in 1977, at age eighty-eight, American astronaut and former Scoutmaster Neil Armstrong had taken a world Scout badge to the moon. B-P's original idea had grown into an international organization with a membership of over thirteen million.

Since Olave Lady Baden-Powell's death the work has gone on. Today, Scouting is a growing, worldwide youth movement with more than sixteen million members (Scouts and Girl Scouts) in 150 countries and territories. The Girl Guides, Olave Lady Baden-Powell's special concern, now total nearly seven-and-a-half million in 112 countries.

Like any living, developing organization, both groups still have problems to face and daily decisions to make. Should the basic uniforms be modernized? Should the Girl Guides and Girl Scouts and the Boy Scouts join together? How can organizations in the West best help the underdeveloped countries? Some are difficult questions of ethics and religious belief: can the Scout Oath and Scout Law be accepted by people of very different faiths or no faith at all?

Thank you, B-P!

Over the past eight decades, the lives of millions of young people all over the world have been changed by the high ideals and wonderful sense of fun of Robert Baden-Powell.

The future can seem daunting, but membership among both girls and boys continues to grow. The movement is confident that the resourceful and innovative attitudes inherited from its founder will carry it on into the twenty-first century.

For More Information . . .

Organizations

The following organizations can provide you with more information about the Boy Scouts, Girl Scouts, and other organizations that are working to give young people recreational and educational opportunities. Some of these groups publish magazines describing their activities, and you may want to subscribe to them. When you write, be sure to tell them exactly what you would like to know, and remember to include your name, address, and age.

American Camping Association, Inc.
5000 State Road, 67 North
Martinsville, IN 46151

Boy Scouts of America
1325 Walnut Hill Lane
P.O. Box 152079
Irving, TX 75015

Boys and Girls Clubs of Canada
250 Consumers Road, Suite 505
Willowdale, Ontario M2J 4V6
Canada

Boys Clubs of America
771 First Avenue
New York, NY 10017

Camp Fire Boys and Girls
4601 Madison Avenue
Kansas City, MO 64112

Canadian Camping Association
1806 Avenue Road, Suite 2
Toronto, Ontario M5M 3Z1
Canada

Girl Guides of Canada
50 Merton Street
Toronto, Ontario M4S 1A3
Canada

Girls Clubs of America
30 East 33rd Street
New York, NY 10016

National Campers and Hikers Association
4804 Transit Road, Building 2
Depew, NY 14043

Scouting for the Handicapped
1325 Walnut Hill Lane
P.O. Box 152079
Irving, TX 75015

For questions about the Girl Scouts of the U.S.A. and about the Boy Scouts of Canada, please call or write to a local council. The telephone number and address can be found in your telephone book.

Magazines

The publications listed below will tell you more about camping and other activities of interest to young people. Check your local library to see if they subscribe to the magazines or write to the addresses listed if you are interested in subscribing.

Boys' Life
1325 Walnut Hill Lane
P.O. Box 152079
Irving, TX 75015

Leadership Magazine
4601 Madison Avenue
Kansas City, MO 64112

Voice for Girls
30 East 33rd Street
New York, NY 10016

For articles specifically about ecology, canoeing, and the outdoors . . .

American Camping Association, Inc.
5000 State Road, 67 North
Martinsville, IN 46151

Canadian Camping Association
1806 Avenue Road, Suite 2
Toronto, Ontario M5M 3Z1
Canada

If you are in the Midwest, you may want to see the Girl Scout and Boy Scout materials on display at . . .

Zitelman Scout Museum
708 Seminary Street
Rockford, Illinois 61104

Books

The books listed below will help you learn more about Scouting as well as the Boy Scouts, Girl Guides, Girl Scouts, and the kinds of activities they promote. Check your library or bookstore to see if they have them or can order them for you.

Baden-Powell, a Family Album. Baden-Powell (A. Sutton)
Baden-Powell, the Two Lives of a Hero. Hillcourt, with Olave, Lady Baden-Powell (Heinemann)
Bicycle Touring and Camping. Dolan (Wanderer Books)
B-P's Scouts, an Official History. Collis, Hazlewood, and Hurll (Collins)
Cub Scout Family Book. (Boy Scouts of America)
Girl Scout Cadet Handbook. (To obtain a copy, check your phone book for the address of the local Girl Scout council.)
Girl Scouts of the U.S.A.: Feeding a Crowd. (Girl Scouts of the U.S.A.)
Story of the Boy Scouts. Blassingame (Garrard)
Round the World: History of Girl Guiding-Girl Scouting. World Association of Girl Guides and Girl Scouts (Girl Scouts of the U.S.A.)
Wildwood Wisdom. Jaeger (Macmillan)

Glossary

Afrikaners
Called *Boers* until the twentieth century, these are South Africans descended from early Dutch settlers. They speak Afrikaans, a language that developed from 17th-century Dutch. This language has become the official language of the Republic of South Africa.

Boer War (1899-1902)
A conflict between the Boers (who came to South Africa in the 17th century) and the British (who arrived in the early nineteenth century). As more English people

moved into South Africa, the Boers resented their presence. Tensions escalated until finally war broke out. The treaty made at the end of the war made the Transvaal and the Orange Free State colonies of the British Empire. In 1910, the British passed the South Africa Act, combining these two conquered Dutch republics with the British Cape Colony. The new country this created, the Union of South Africa, was then given its independence. In 1961, the country, renamed the Republic of South Africa, withdrew from the British Commonwealth.

cavalry

A part of an army which is made up of soldiers on horseback or in vehicles.

impi

A group of Zulu warriors. The Zulu are members of the Bantu nation, a group that includes many tribes living in southern and central Africa.

infantry

A branch of an army that is trained to fight on foot.

jamboree

Although it originally referred to a noisy drinking bout or merrymaking, this word is more commonly used to refer to large groups of Scouts gathered for meetings, exhibits, and celebration.

reconnaissance

The inspection or exploration of an area in order to get information about an enemy or the area.

scout

In military terms, a person who is sent out to observe and obtain information about an enemy or about the land. But with a capital letter, as *Scout*, this term has come to refer to a young person who is a member of Baden-Powell's movement.

totalitarian

A word used to describe a government led by a single leader or group that regulates every aspect of people's lives. Those in power allow no other political parties.

yarn

A long, involved story of exciting or incredible events, fictional or real. When presenting a yarn, storytellers may spin out events differently with each retelling.

Chronology

1857   February 22 — Robert Powell is born in London.

1860   Baden Powell, Robert's father, dies. He was a well-known scientist as well as a clergyman.

1869   The family name is changed from Powell to Baden-Powell.

1870   B-P, as he is known, wins a scholarship to Charterhouse, in Surrey.

1876   Baden-Powell, age nineteen, joins the 13th Hussars (a top cavalry regiment in the British army) and begins service in India.

1878	B-P is promoted to the rank of lieutenant, becomes ill, and is sent to England on sick leave.
1880	B-P returns to active service in India and takes part in the Afghan War.
1884	B-P, now twenty-seven, serves with the British army in Africa. He publishes his first book, *Reconnaissance and Scouting*.
1897	Now a colonel, Baden-Powell returns to India, where he develops new training methods for his men.
1899	With the outbreak of the Boer War, Baden-Powell is sent to South Africa. **October** — The town of Mafeking falls under siege, with Baden-Powell in charge of its defense. Seven months later, when the town is relieved by British troops, he becomes a national hero.
1900	B-P, age forty-three, becomes the youngest major general in the British army.
1901	Queen Victoria dies after sixty-three years as the British monarch. B-P forms the South African Constabulary, a mounted police force with the motto "Be Prepared."
1903	Baden-Powell returns to England as inspector general of cavalry and spends the next four years trying to adapt his Indian and African experiences into a solution for the problem of growing juvenile delinquency among boys.
1907	B-P is promoted to lieutenant general and retires from active duty. He takes the first group of young boys to camp at Brownsea Island.
1908	B-P publishes the first Scout handbook, *Scouting for Boys*, as well as a weekly magazine, *The Scout*, and organizes the second Scout camp.
1909	The Crystal Palace rally takes place, with about 11,000 Scouts attending. The first girls seek to join the Scouting movement. B-P becomes Sir Robert Baden-Powell.
1910	Baden-Powell, age fifty-three, resigns from the army to devote himself to Scouting. There are now more than 100 thousand Scouts and the movement is catching on in other countries. B-P's sister, Agnes Baden-Powell, forms the Girl Guides in England. In the United States, William Boyce founds the Boy Scouts of America. Dr. Luther Halsey Gulick starts a sister organization, which is known as the Camp Fire Girls.
1912	At age fifty-five, Baden-Powell meets and marries Olave Soames. Juliette Gordon Low starts the Girl Scouts of the U.S.A., basing the organization on the Girl Guides in England. This group, like its counterparts in other nations, is part of the World Association of Girl Guides and Girl Scouts (WAGGGS).
1913	Peter, the first of the Baden-Powell children, is born.
1915	Heather Baden-Powell is born.

1917	Betty Baden-Powell is born.

1917 Betty Baden-Powell is born.

1918 Olave Baden-Powell reorganizes the Girl Guides and is elected chief guide. Her title is changed to "World Chief Guide" in 1930.

1919 The family moves to Pax Hill, Hampshire, England.

1920 The first World Jamboree is held at Olympia, London, with Scouts from twenty-one countries and twelve colonies of the British Empire attending. B-P is acclaimed as "Chief Scout of the World."

1924 The second World Jamboree is held in Denmark.

1927 Italian dictator Benito Mussolini bans Scouting in Italy and replaces the organization with his own nationalist youth organizations.

1929 The Coming-of-Age World Jamboree takes place and there are now almost two million Scouts worldwide.
King George V makes B-P Lord Baden-Powell of Gilwell.

1930-31 The Baden-Powells visit the West Indies, New York, New Zealand, Australia, and South Africa.

1933 Scouts celebrate the fourth World Jamboree in Hungary.
Baden-Powell has a serious operation but recovers. Over the next few years, B-P visits Australia, the United States, and other nations with Scout troops. Adolf Hitler bans Scouting in Germany and replaces the organization with militant German youth organizations.

1937 B-P celebrates his eightieth birthday.
He attends the fifth World Jamboree and receives the Carnegie Prize for his services to world peace and for promoting international goodwill.

1938 The Baden-Powells retire to Paxtu, their new home in Africa.

1939 **June** — A census shows 3,305,149 Scouts in forty-seven countries.

1941 **January 8** — Lord Robert Baden-Powell dies at Paxtu at age eighty-three.

1946 Scouting is restored in Germany and Italy.

1977 Olave Lady Baden-Powell dies at age eighty-eight.

1990 The most recent figures show over twenty-three million Boy Scouts, Girl Scouts, and Girl Guides in 150 countries and territories. The numbers increase yearly.

The Scout Motto

Be prepared.

The Scout Slogan

Do a good turn daily.

The Three Aspects of the Scout Code of Living

A spiritual dimension — the commitment to seek the spiritual value of life beyond the material world.

A social dimension — the obligation to participate in the development of society, to respect the dignity of others and the integrity of the natural world; and to promote local, national, and international peace, understanding, and cooperation.

A personal dimension — the desire to develop a sense of personal responsibility and attain responsible self-expression.

The Scout Oath or Promise

I promise on my honour
1. To do my duty to God and the King.
2. To help other people at all times.
3. To obey the Scout Law.

(original British version)

I give my word of honor
that I will do my best
1. To do my duty to God and the country.
2. To help other people at all times.
3. To obey the Scout Law.

(version written by Baden-Powell for U.S. in 1910)

On my honor
I will do my best
To do my duty to God
  and my country and
To obey the Scout Law;
To help other people
  at all times;
To keep myself physically strong,
  Mentally awake, and morally straight.

(current U.S. version, adopted in 1911)

The Outdoor Code

As an American, I will do my best to be clean in my outdoor manners, be careful with fire, be considerate in the outdoors, and be conservation-minded.

The Scout Law

A Scout is . . . Trustworthy
Loyal
Helpful
Friendly
Courteous
Kind
Obedient
Cheerful
Thrifty
Brave
Clean
Reverent

An American Cub Scout proudly displays the birdhouse he built for his family. Near his waist hangs a string of beads. Each bead represents the number of points he has earned by learning new skills and performing services for others.

Index

Baden-Powell, Agnes 25, 36-37

Baden-Powell, Heather 42, 43, 49, 52

Baden-Powell, Olave St. Clair Soames 36, 40-41, 42-43, 44-45, 48, 49, 51-52, 53, 56, 57-58, 59-60

Baden-Powell, Robert: as "Chief Scout of the World" 46, 48, 55; childhood of 4-10; and concern for wayward young men 26-27, 44; death of 55; education of 6, 9-11; farewell messages of 50, 52-53, 56, 60; as father 42-43; and girls in the Scouting movement 36-38; as hero of siege of Mafeking 17-27, 29; as international Scout leader 38, 40, 42-43, 44, 45-48, 49-53, 55-56; knighting of 40; as lecturer 30; as Lord Baden-Powell of Gilwell 48-49; and love of nature 4-7, 56, 58; as military leader 11-26, 27, 40; and the origins of the Scouting movement 26-32; talents of 4, 9, 11, 12, 33, 42, 43, 44, 52, 53; Zulu names for 15

Boer War 16-26

Boy Scouts of America 38, 40, 57

Boyce, William 38

Brownsea Island 28, 29-31, 32, 48, 54

Charterhouse 4, 5, 6, 7, 9, 10

"Chief Scout of the World" 46, 48, 55

CITIES: Bentley, England 44; Bombay, India 13; Durban, South Africa 49; Geneva, Switzerland 58; Kimberley, South Africa 17; Kingston, Jamaica 41; London, England 24, 25, 32, 36, 38, 40, 45, 55, 56, 58; Mafeking, South Africa 17-25, 26, 27, 29, 53; New Delhi, India 58; Nyeri, Kenya 53, 55; Ottawa, Canada 58; Paris, France 52

Copse, The 4-5, 7, 9, 12, 59

COUNTRIES: Afghanistan 12; Algeria 42; Australia 38, 42, 52, 56; Austria 56; Belgium 40; Brunei 46; Canada 11, 38, 40, 52, 58; Chile 38; China 42; Cyprus 46; Denmark 38; Dominica 46; England (*see* Great Britain); Finland 38; France 15, 38, 56; Germany 50, 56; Great Britain 5, 6, 11, 12, 14, 15, 26, 29, 32, 38, 44, 49, 50, 56; Greece 38; Guyana 38; Holland 38, 40, 45, 49, 52; Hungary 49; India 10, 11, 12, 13, 15, 16, 27, 29, 32, 38, 48, 49, 56, 57, 58, 59; Italy 50-51, 56; Jamaica 38, 41; Japan 42, 45; Luxembourg 56; New Guinea 42; New Zealand 38, 42, 46; Philippines 58; Singapore 38; South Africa 14-15, 16, 17, 18, 23, 25, 26, 38, 42, 48, 49-50, 51, 52, 55; Soviet Union 38; Sri Lanka 38; Switzerland 58; Thailand 45; United States of America 11, 38, 40, 42, 56; Zimbabwe 38

Girl Guides and Girl Scouts 36, 37, 38, 41, 43, 44, 49, 50, 52, 53, 55, 56, 57, 58, 60

Hitler, Adolf 50

Jamborees 44, 45-48, 49, 51-53, 55, 56, 58

Mafeking Cadet Corps 21-23

Mafeking, Siege of (*see* Siege of Mafeking)

Mussolini, Benito 50-51

Nagy, Laszlo 48, 56, 57, 60

Pax Hill 44, 48, 49, 53

Paxtu 53, 55, 56

PEOPLES: Africans 29; American Indians 5-6, 28; Americans 38, 45; Arabs 59; Boers 16, 17, 18, 19; British 5, 7, 13, 16, 17, 23, 24, 25, 36, 40, 45, 49, 50; Canadians 49; Dutch 16, 45; French 52; Germans 50, 56; Irish 48; Italians 56; Japanese 56, 59; Kenyans 56; Zulu 13-15, 29

Powell, Baden 7

Powell, Henrietta 6, 7-9, 41, 42

Scout badges 15-16, 32, 35, 43

Scout Law 31-32, 35, 53, 60

Scout Motto 29, 38, 43

Scout Oath or Promise 31-32, 35, 60

Scout Slogan 40

Scout uniform 15, 29, 32, 35

Siege of Mafeking 17-25

West, James E. 57

World War I 38, 43, 44

World War II 50, 52, 56